ANIMAL COLORING BOOK

This Book Belongs To

COLOR TEST PAGE

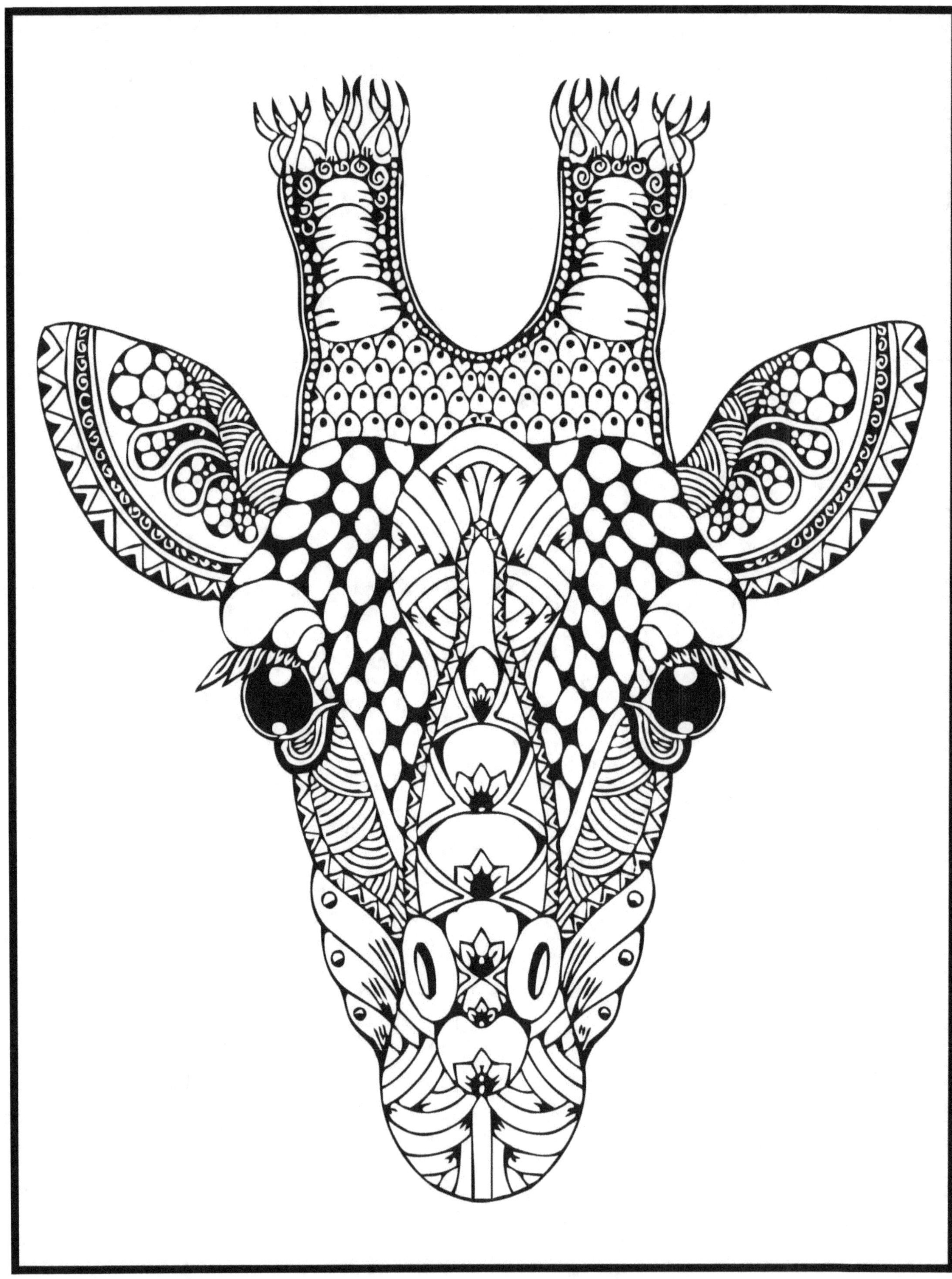

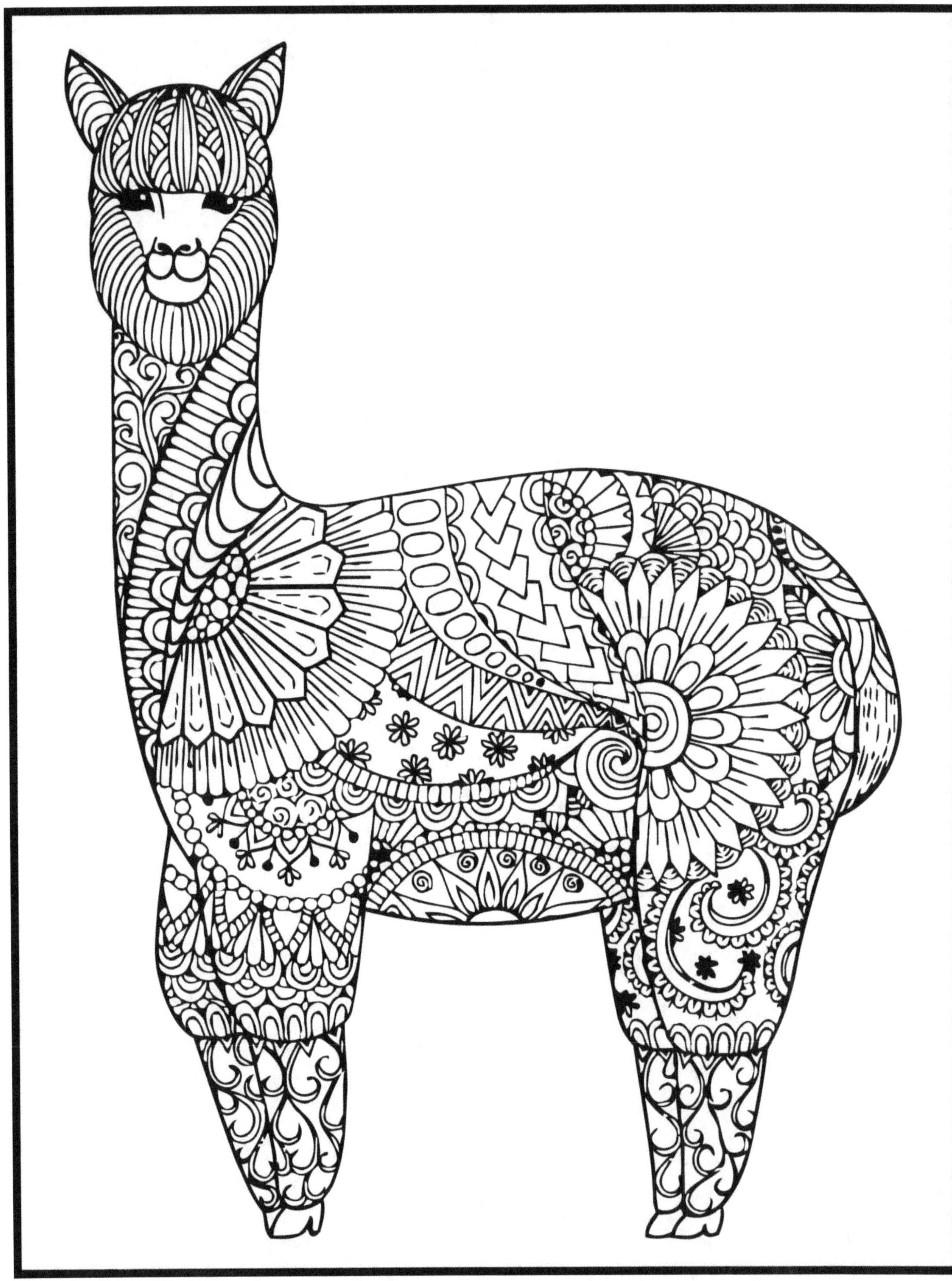

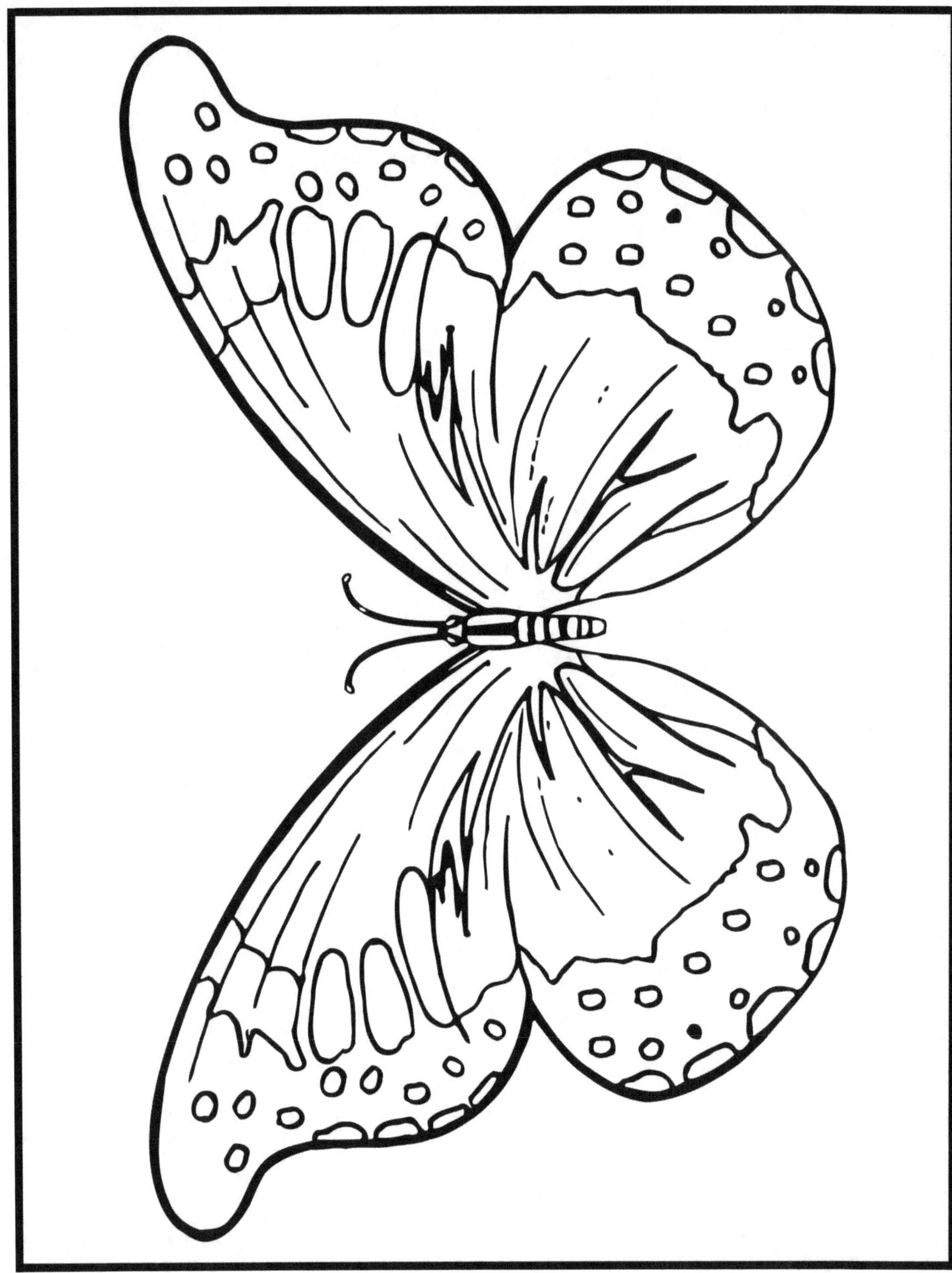

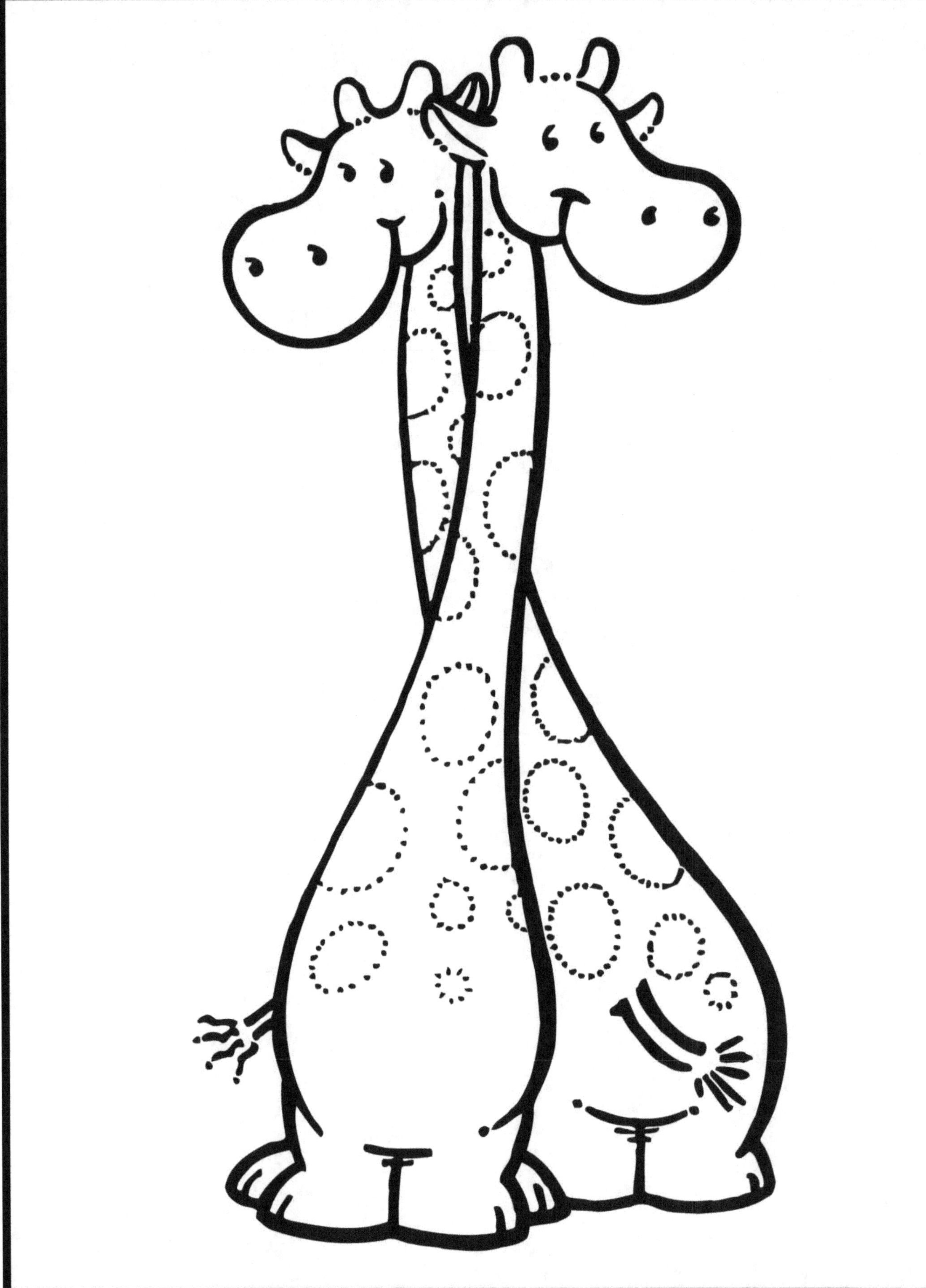

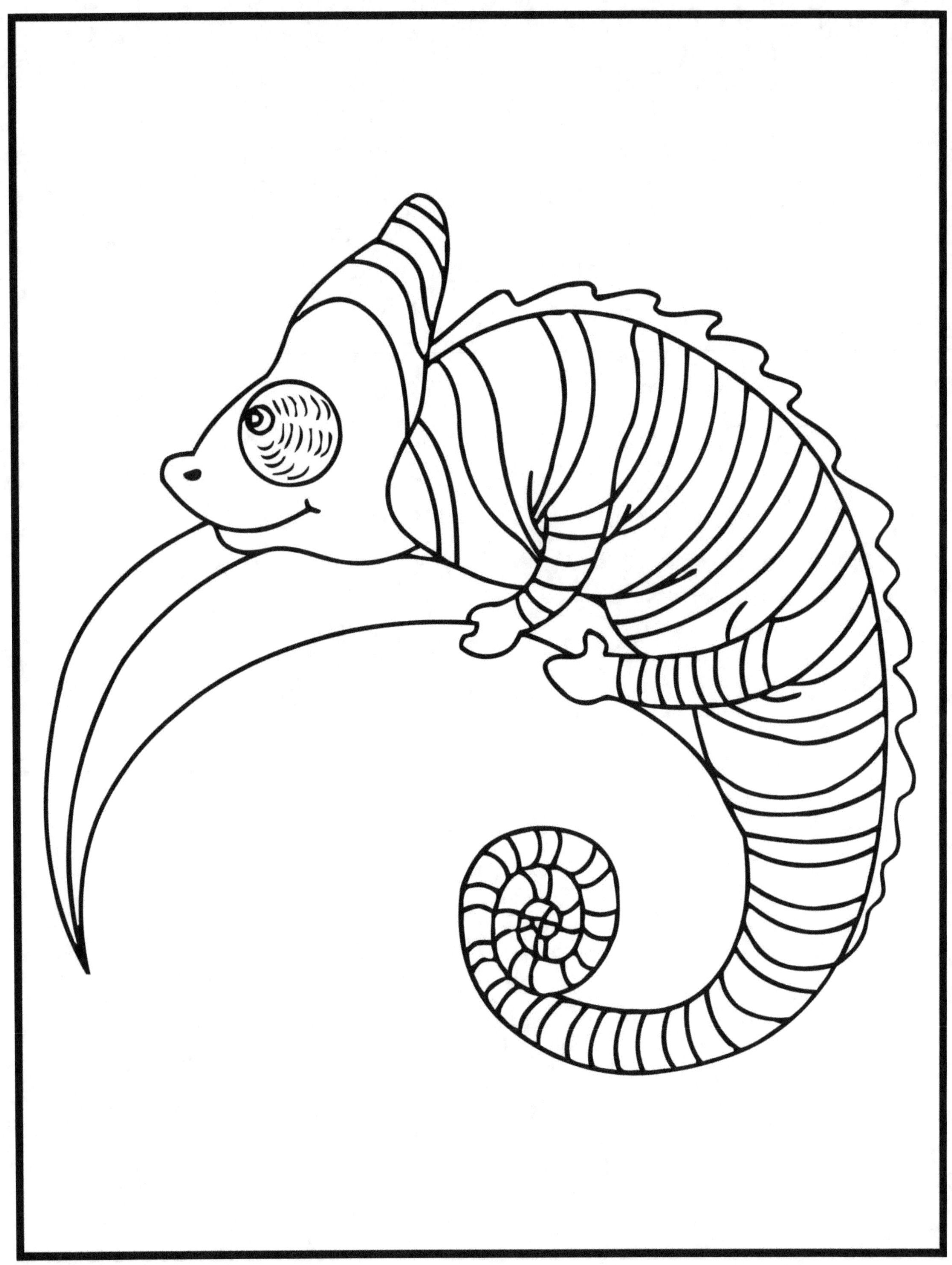

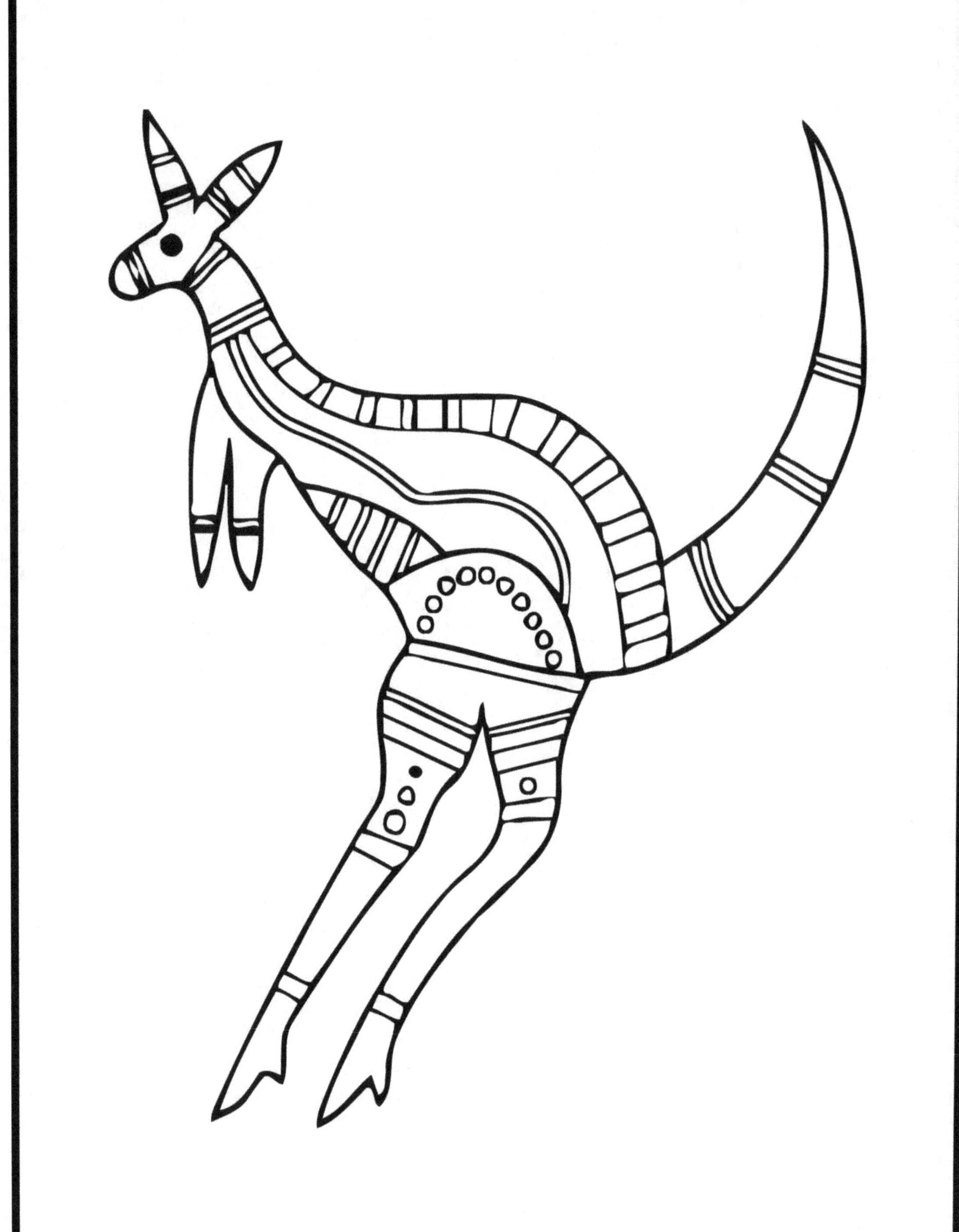

www.ingramcontent.com/pod-product-compliance
Lightning Source LLC
Chambersburg PA
CBHW081441250726
48662CB00009B/2889